CONSCIOUSLY
Beautiful

I AM ENOUGH

ARDRE ORIE

Consciously Beautiful

ISBN: 978-0-9916015-1-6 (Value Edition)

ACKNOWLEDGEMENTS

Nothing monumental can be achieved alone. A heartfelt expression of gratitude to all of the amazing people that helped to make this book a success:

PHOTOGRAPHY

LEAD PHOTOGRAPHER:
Kevin Dukes
www.kdukesphoto.com

ASSISTING PHOTOGRAPHER/CREATIVE DIRECTOR:
Alima Albari
www.alimaindustries.com

CONTRIBUTING PHOTOGRAPHERS:
Tim Rogers, TWR Photography
www.twrphotography.com
Quadir Thomas, Mecca1 Photography
www.mecca1photos.com

MAKEUP

I Love Me
www.ilovemeglam.com
www.ilovemeorganics.com

HAIR

On behalf of the Consciously Beautiful family, we would like to thank Salon Greco, the European Salon and Day Spa for being the 2013 Hair Sponsor of the Consciously Beautiful Retreat. Your kindness will be long remembered.

Salon Greco
www.salongreco.com

DEDICATION

This book is dedicated to those who make my breaths worth taking and give me moments that take my breath away:

Acceptance
Honesty
Love

I met you when I was 14. I always knew that you were sent to me by God. Time and the elements of self-discovery would eventually separate us, but no force can change the will of the universe.

You have given me the power to believe that I am beautiful. You have accepted me for who I am even in times when I did not accept myself. You healed my hurt and gave me hope. I am a dreamer, and hope is the fuel that breathes life into my existence. I am the woman that I am because of you.

Confidence
Charisma
Life

Being born on your birthday was the greatest gift that the creator could have given to me besides his love and forgiveness, for he gifted me with a pure soul who would understand the very essence of me. All we strive for in life is to be understood. Through every moment of my life, you have been there by my side faithfully. You taught me the meaning of what a mother is and should be, and I can only hope that I will be as influential in the lives of my children as you have been in mine. I can never repay you for your heart's love, but I promise with every bone in my body to pay if forward. I am powerful because you told me that I was. I achieve because you told me that I could. I am because you are.

MY CHILDREN:

Bold

Fearless

Future

Shamon, Lauren and London, you must always remember that you are smart and beautiful. Never forget your dreams that we often speak of, never forget the power that you have, never forget to love yourself, for I love you with every breath, every heartbeat and every moment in time. You complete me.

FOREWORD

Whether through pain or prosperity,

every face has a *story to tell*.

Our stories shape who we are and

what we *give to the world*.

In my eyes, the term "beautiful" has always been about the effect that we
have on others. Beauty draws people to action, evokes emotions and creates
an awareness in the viewer that makes an imprint in one's mind. Being beautiful is an art. I have always wanted so desperately to create beautiful things
in the world simply because that is what I see. I feel most beautiful when
creating, giving, learning and becoming. It seems, however, as though these
behaviors we most associate with struggle.

Beauty in our world is immediately classified by what is visible to the eye.
This is not a foreign pattern of thought as our brains decipher information.
The only information that we have initially is what we see. We are told to
never judge a book by its cover and to see people for who they are, but this

is virtually impossible because we don't have that information. The world has taught us to love what we are told is beautiful and shun everything else. We spend countless hours trying to live up to an incomparable standard. It's almost as if we are puppets on a string being controlled. With awareness, we awaken and understand that the things that make us different are the things that make us beautiful. It took me some time to find comfort in this sentiment because I often just wanted to be like everyone else. Being different also means being subjected to ostracism, isolation, bullying and sometimes self-hate.

We must intensely examine the motives that drive our opinions, thoughts and sentiments about beauty. We must open our eyes, we must be awakened, we must become conscious. We must learn to filter images and subliminal messages from newspapers, magazines, radio, television and social media that continue to drive us towards the destruction of ourselves due to comparison.

We must return our focus and our actions towards kindness of the heart as the hierarchy for the measure of beauty.

We must be or become *Consciously Beautiful*

INTRODUCTION

$\mathcal{A}$ journey is defined as an act of traveling from one place to another. I believe that the best visual for this is the dash that represents the years between birth and death.

My beautiful journey began as a little four-year-old girl in a single-parent home who would get all dressed up and sit by the window waiting for my father to visit. I was met with disappointment as he would often never arrive at my door. At the time, I had no understanding or reference of his reasoning and was left only to believe that I was not loved by him. I traveled through life masking the sadness and believing that the world was to be consumed in isolation. I never felt that I measured up. In retrospect, I would later learn that the standard to which I had been holding myself accountable never truly existed.

The certainty that I possessed in myself was an ability to turn pain into passion and help others to see the beauty in themselves. I can remember making over friends, teachers, and family members in their homes from as early as age ten. In a recent conversation, my mother reminded me of how many adult women would visit our home to have their hair done by me and that I have been in the business of beauty all of my life. There was something so profound about the look on a woman's face when she felt beautiful.

My journey would later lead me to educating students, where I witnessed the disparity between students who were confident in their ability to achieve versus the incompetence of students who did not believe themselves to be capable. I gleaned that there was a tremendous energy associated with how we feel about ourselves. I knew that I had to do more to inspire, uplift, and help others discover their beauty, so I launched the Pink Wish Foundation, a 501(c)(3) organization with a mission to empower women and girls through economic independence and leadership. Throughout my work with young ladies as well as their mothers, I reveled in the fact that no matter how much we learned about financial stability, we were all most happy when we felt good about ourselves. Each of the families that I worked with demonstrated year after year that there was a direct correlation between the way we feel about ourselves and what we can achieve.

A year prior to writing this book, I launched I Love Me, a cosmetics company, and began more work with women through photo shoots and new product launches. I was now a bona fide beauty industry professional and surrounded by beautiful people. In the midst of this environment, my sentiments shifted from a simple thought process to the following hypothesis: If we are not happy with the person that we see in the mirror, our potential to learn, grow, and execute is stifled. Furthermore, when we make decisions from this perspective, we often settle for far less than what we deserve and operate from an oppressed disposition. Throughout my journey, I have always made less than stellar decisions about what I was capable of and who I truly was when I channeled the "you are not good enough," "fatherless" voice. I was moved to action. I knew that through my previous work with the Pink Wish Foundation as well as I Love Me, I had an audience of women and teen girls who needed to be reminded that their worth rested in their ability to see it. *Consciously Beautiful: I Am Enough* is my act of desperation to scream from the rooftops to every ear that will hear that, no matter what circumstances we are given or what the world tells us about beauty, we must find the strength to love ourselves. This is the only true way to harness the energy and greatness that lies within us all.

I set out on a mission, to find ladies whose stories needed to be told, women whose voices needed to be heard and we gathered in love for what would become the 1st Annual Consciously Beautiful Weekend Retreat. Within the first five minutes of sharing our stories, we were inspired, moved to tears and relieved simultaneously. We determined that if we were going to speak about our internal struggles, trials and triumphs, we were going to hold no bars. We would tell our stories in such a way that any person who picked up the book would find at least one story, sentiment, or struggle that they could relate to or be engaged with.

This book is not written through the eyes of someone wearing rose-colored glasses; it is raw and, most importantly, genuine. The pain, hurt, and happiness that is described in these pages are meant to evoke emotion. The pendulum of stories swings from happy, confident lives to lives impacted by skin bleaching, eating disorders and drug abuse. No matter the story, the theme that emerged spoke loud and clear: We have an internal need to be accepted by ourselves and by others. Additionally, I was enlightened to the many added burdens we accept from the world that truly impact our thoughts of self, such as mainstream media, social media, and even loved ones.

In reflection, I believe that there is nothing pretty about the beautiful journey, for what lies at the end of the road is often uncertain. We can, however, find strength and comfort in knowing that the journey is art and the destination—the person we see in the mirror—is simply a masterpiece.

CONTENTS

CONSCIOUSLY
Beautiful

MELISSA

Too often we *aspire* to be

what we think we are supposed to be

and not what we *truly want to be*.

Have you ever been told that your scars make you beautiful? I happen to believe that my scars are absolutely breathtaking. I proudly display scars from the emotional and physical triumphs that have helped to define my beautiful journey.

I am German, Jewish, and absolutely comfortable with the skin I'm in. This was not always the case. Growing up, I enjoyed many activities that were considered "tomboyish," and I never really had the opportunity to unleash my inner girl. In the seventh grade, I began to pay more attention to my body and was not in love with what I saw. I became anorexic and would only bring a rice cake to eat at lunch. I was not skinny and I, like most women, believed that skinny was synonymous with beautiful.

In high school, I felt like I was passed over by guys and was destined for the friend lane. I never felt comfortable expressing my inner struggle because, in true tomboy fashion, I had no reason to obsess over girly issues. When I did have a boyfriend, I spent much of my relationship in paranoia due to my own insecurities. If I thought that my boyfriend was checking out another girl, I would get upset. If I saw another girl that I believed to be pretty, I would get upset and accuse him of checking her out. I was trapped by my thoughts and disapproval of myself.

As time went on, I made decisions that I would later regret with sexual partners who were not worthy of me. I know this to be the case with many women. If we truly knew our worth, there would be an extreme value placed on the offering of ourselves, and we simply wouldn't do so with men who are less than deserving.

In 2001, I was involved in a head-on collision. I died and was revived. After being bound to a wheelchair for four months, my beautiful journey took a detour. My face showcased a beautiful scar that would define me as unique. For the first time in my life, I really felt beautiful.

Life has taught me many things, but among the most important is this: People should feel whatever it is that they feel. We shouldn't tell them not to. It devalues what they might be going through. I have also given people permission to judge and given myself permission to not care if I am misjudged.

I want to encourage every woman to find one thing that they like about themselves and become fascinated with it. My bet is that when you can find one thing that you love about yourself, you will discover many more.

Too often we aspire to be what we think we are supposed to be and not what we truly want to be. The images of beauty that we see in popular media are not real. We spend too much time chasing a false reality.

You are allowed to prejudge me. Should your judgments result in ignorance, it defines you; it does not define me.

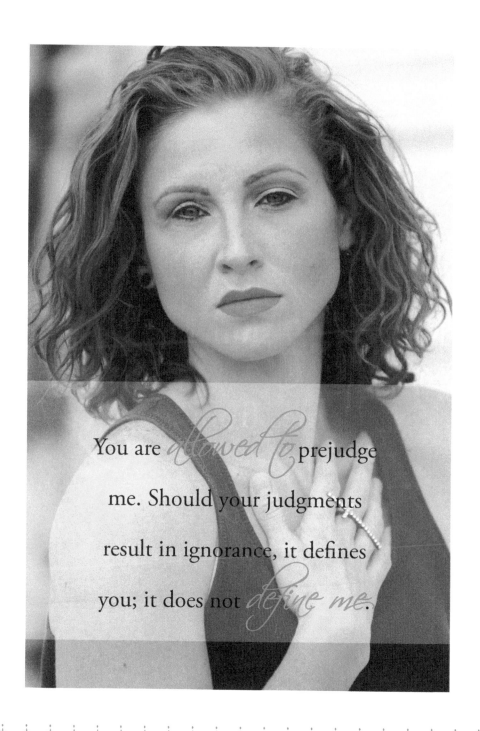

You are *allowed to* prejudge me. Should your judgments result in ignorance, it defines you; it does not *define me.*

My *light* shines because it comes from *within.*

~ ARDRE ORIE

CONSCIOUSLY *Beautiful* THOUGHTS

ARIANA

My *beautiful* journey

has yielded an amazing sense

of confidence and made me

extremely proud

to be just as I am.

I am not sick, I will not wear a wig, and I am not sorry that I am bald.

My family is composed of a number of beautiful races, although I am mainly black and Filipino. I see all people as beautiful and am extremely proud of my mixed heritage. My beautiful journey began as a long-haired, enthusiastic kid who had love and luster for life. My hair was waist-long and the moment I began losing it was the moment that my beautiful journey embarked upon an unexpected trail, one that I would later blaze. I was diagnosed with alopecia, a hereditary autoimmune disorder that causes hair loss. There are times when I have no eyelashes or eyebrows as a result of the alopecia, and I sense that others are uncomfortable by it.

In general, there are times when people question and are often uncomfortable with the beauty of others. My diagnosis caused me to rethink my entire concept of beauty.

I am beautifully bald because I have alopecia. Although racially ambiguous, I have been discriminated against, but found that to be the lesser challenge. Many people are eager to jump towards sympathy because I am a bald, young woman. I've never needed sympathy because I make no apologies for what I feel is beautiful. It seems to me that the rest of the world needs sympathy because we are often too blind to see real beauty due to the constant images and comparisons fed to us by the media, as well as those that are a direct result of our own insecurities.

I have come to embrace my *beauty* for what it is and what it is not.

I have discovered that the only time I become insecure is when I compare my beauty to someone else's. Many women are not comfortable in their own skin or have low self-esteem, which is often a byproduct of the unnecessary comparisons that we make. My beautiful journey has yielded an amazing sense of confidence and made me extremely proud to be just as I am. It is with this confidence that I hope to inspire others to embrace their beauty.

I have come to embrace my beauty for what it is and what it is not.

Words say very little when eyes *speak loud* and clear.

~ ARDRE ORIE

CONSCIOUSLY *Beautiful* THOUGHTS

MIRIAH

Because I *love myself*, I no longer

allow others to treat me in

ways that don't encourage

me to *embrace my beauty*.

I will never forget the day at school when a girl yelled across the gym in front of several people that she would give me $1 to clean her house. Growing up I was bullied and ridiculed with names like "wetback" and "half-breed." I would allow the actions of bullies to become my truth and allow them to manifest in my low self-esteem. I can still hear the voice of a girl whom I befriended say, "My mommy and daddy said I cannot play with you." These comments became patchwork in the quilt of my beautiful journey. In my city, there is only white and black. If you are not white, then pretty much you are considered black. My father is Mexican and my mother is white.

I wanted nothing more than to have blonde hair and blue eyes. This was my idea of beauty. I rejected myself to the point that I began to reject the world and people around me as well. I began to blame the world and myself for what I had experienced and why others did not see me as pretty. I began to mistreat my older siblings and stray from my faith. I wanted my skin to be lighter such to the point that I would avoid going outside to protect my skin from the sun.

Around this time, the United States was dealing with many issues concerning immigration, and my peers would even ask, "Where is your green card?" I determined that if I did not make a decision to speak up, who would?

After my quinceañera (the traditional Latin American celebration of a girl's fifteenth birthday), I began to accept myself. I became proud of who I was. I determined that there was no fun in being normal. My beautiful journey took me to a stop of empowerment: In my senior year of high school, I became the president of the Spanish club and began speaking to other young ladies like me, telling them that they are beautiful and explaining the importance of loving themselves. My beautiful journey now had purpose.

I currently spend a great deal of my time supporting young ladies and encouraging them that if I can find confidence, then they have every reason to. I have grown to love myself and others.

"Everyone is *beautiful*, everyone

has *flaws*, flaws are beautiful

and *beauty is flawed*."

Because I love myself, I no longer allow others to treat me in ways that don't encourage me to embrace my beauty. I embrace myself and my flaws because I am so proud to be exactly who I am.

My beautiful journey revealed my inner power and my willingness to advocate and empower other young ladies. I feel most beautiful when I am making a difference.

"Everyone is beautiful, everyone has flaws, flaws are beautiful and beauty is flawed."

My *beauty* can open a door of opportunity but it is without question my *heart* that has the *power* to open the windows of the *world.*

~ ARDRE ORIE

CONSCIOUSLY *Beautiful* THOUGHTS

DEANNA

The depth of my skin reveals
a *beautiful winding road* of
heritage, courage, and wisdom.

he depth of my skin reveals a beautiful winding road of heritage, courage, and wisdom. My beautiful journey begins with my Mexican, Guatemalan, and American lineage. I was born in California and believe with my entire heart that our differences make each of us unique and beautiful. At some point, every girl or woman has felt a sense of insecurity about their external beauty. There are so many negative messages that surround us that we can often feel persuaded to make comparisons and be like everyone else.

I have made it a priority to understand who I am through understanding my family.

When I was younger my family called me "Negra." This is a Spanish term meaning "dark." My mother was also referred to by this name. I did not know why my skin color was used to categorize me and often felt that I was being made fun of. At times, I would be moved to tears because I did not truly accept my darker complexion. I later learned that my family meant this as a term of endearment, and I have learned to embrace my darker skin complexion. Other Hispanics have a darker skin color like me, and I believe it to be beautiful.

At about age seven, my beautiful journey took an interesting turn on a street called confidence. I remember feeling pretty. I became passionate about posing for pictures and pleased with the way that I looked and felt when doing so. I wanted to be a model. At age 12, I began researching the modeling industry.

Even though I believe myself to possess high self-esteem, I, like every other teen my age, have areas in which I question myself. I have always been concerned about my height. Additionally, I find that people are often confused about my race. I have learned to take the characteristics that make me unique and use them to my advantage.

I determined that I would work as a print model, which would empower me to not be concerned about my height.

Many people think my race is Indian, American Indian, or that I'm mixed with African American. Through my research and agents, I have learned that I can portray different heritages in my modeling and acting career.

My beautiful journey has taught me that there will always be someone saying negative things about you. The goal should be to love ourselves past the hurt that words can cause. I have learned to place greater value on compliments that reference my ability to make others smile than those that reference my physical attributes.

No longer do I compare myself to models on TV or in magazines only to discover my flaws; that is pointless. Instead, I use photographs to motivate me and learn poses and acting strategies.

If I could, I would inspire my younger sister and other young ladies to accept themselves for who they truly are, because we are all amazingly beautiful in a certain way, even if most times we don't realize it. I encourage women and girls to know our weak points, grow from them, and always keep our heads held high.

The goal should be to *love ourselves* past the hurt that words can cause.

It is my hope that my beautiful journey will lead me to a college degree and a modeling/acting career. When I look into the mirror, I see a 14-year-old girl that knows what she wants for herself and the goals she wants to reach. I am learning to love myself more and more each day.

I am *simply* beautiful.
I simply believe in my ability to
make the world a better place.
I simply know that I can
make a difference. That is
simply *beautiful*.

~ ARDRE ORIE

CONSCIOUSLY *Beautiful* THOUGHTS

REGAN

If I have the chance to *help someone*, then I want to know that I *gave it* my all and didn't hold anything *back*..

When we strive to please others, we often lose the very essence of ourselves. For so many years, I felt like I didn't have a voice, and I have spent a great deal of my life searching for it. I am still searching for it.

Like many women and girls, I spent much of my high school years struggling with my weight. Although a low point, I did discover a love for performing on stage. Through drama, I found a voice—I found acceptance—and when on stage, I seemed to forget about the rest of the world. Upon graduation, I felt boyish, weighing 200 pounds.

As a result of the negative feelings about myself and social anxiety, I engaged in self-destructive behaviors. My first year of college was tumultuous. I began drinking, made bad grades, took drugs, and I was raped. I engaged in cutting: the only reminder that I was still alive. As the whisper of depression turned into a roar, thoughts of suicide were consistent. I attempted to take my life four times.

The self-destruction continued; I developed an eating disorder and starved myself, losing over 60 pounds. Reflecting on the past, I just wanted to hear the words, "I love you."

As a way to make money, I became an exotic dancer. The stage was still a place with which I associated positive feelings and acceptance. On stage, I felt loved. I felt accepted.

To date, I struggle with social anxiety and try to force self-confidence, but it is often disingenuous. I've attempted counseling, but the truth remains that a difference cannot be made unless you are willing to change the way you see yourself.

Even through all of this, when I look in the mirror, I see beauty. I see eyes filled with pain, joy, and a story that belongs only to me. My story is the essence of who I am. My pain has led me to love the reflection that I see in the mirror.

Although I am still searching for my voice, I have developed a resistance towards caring so deeply about what others think. I am still working on loving me first. I've learned that many times things get worse before they get better. I want women and girls to know what I have been through and know that I survived. If I can make it, I know that someone somewhere going through something similar can make it too.

I need for women and girls everywhere to know that they are someone's reason to live. They are someone's reason to wake up in the morning. Never give up on yourself because the world needs you. Give yourself a chance to live, to experience, to share.

Give yourself a chance to *live*, to *experience*, to *share*. You are or will be somebody's reason to *smile*.

If I have the chance to help someone, then I want to know that I gave it my all and didn't hold anything back.

It is comforting to know that you are not alone when you are going through something. Someone somewhere has gone through something similar to you and they survived.

You are or will be somebody's reason to smile.

Isn't she *lovely?* That is what I say to myself when *I look in* the mirror. I won't wait on the *world* to tell me so.

~ ARDRE ORIE

CONSCIOUSLY *Beautiful* THOUGHTS

KRISTAL

I find great *confidence* in knowing

that I can appreciate

my *natural beauty*

as it is.

$\mathcal{G}$rowing up in a small town often leaves little room for standing out or being different. In school, I was bullied for having curly hair, freckles, and light eyes. Although these features seem normal, it is my belief that people can find anything to make you feel inferior if you allow them to.

By the time I reached the 7th grade, I felt overweight and had thoughts of not eating to be thin.

I continued to work extremely hard to fit into the crowd, and it never worked. I allowed my surroundings to affect me to the point of becoming neurologically ill. My illness resulted in me being in and out of the hospital for about five months. During this time, it became increasingly harder for me to develop positive relationships with others, and the amount of understanding or sympathy for me from others did not increase.

My mother and I made a decision to reroute and embark upon the journey of homeschooling. This change in course proved to be an amazing decision along my beautiful journey. I was not only in a positive environment but on track to graduate early. My journey took another amazing turn when I participated in an acting showcase in front of agents, which led to me being booked six months later. I realized without question that I had something beautiful to share with the world.

In the midst of it all, I've always loved my eyes. I find great confidence in knowing that I can appreciate my natural beauty as it is.

Unique beauty to me is when you walk by someone and can't help but take another look at them, not because of what we see but how they see themselves. It's out of the ordinary type of beauty. I believe when you walk around in confidence and people can see that, you get noticed.

I am now in the movie Holy Matrimony playing a character named Josie Roberts. She has learned to make the best of bad situations and realizes her mistakes.

I now see *beauty* when I look in the *mirror*. There is no one out there *like* me.

I now see beauty when I look in the mirror. Before I used to be a girl with a million mistakes on her face and body. I look at myself now and know that there is no one out there like me.

Like a porcelain doll,
my *beauty* is to be
admired. It could never
be duplicated. There is
only one me.

~ ARDRE ORIE

CONSCIOUSLY *Beautiful* THOUGHTS

TAJUANDA

My light is in *bringing light* to the world.

*T*he thought of considering myself beautiful brings tears to my eyes. For so long fair skin has epitomized beauty; and dark skin, the opposite. I never felt pretty, beautiful, celebrated, or loved, and I never loved the reflection that I saw in the mirror.

I was born in Kentucky but, as a military brat, spent a great deal of my life in Hawaii. I would always hear people say, "You're cute to be dark skinned." Although young, I never felt that to be a genuine compliment.

I was a true tomboy and did not always do all of the girly things that some other girls did. These elements became the backdrop to my beautiful journey.

In school, I was teased constantly by my peers for the color of my skin. Around this time, a movie titled "New Jack City" was popular. One of its characters was very dark in complexion, but this character wasn't attractive; in fact, he was meant to be quite the opposite—a strung-out crack addict. His name was "Pookie."

This is what my classmates began to call me: "Pookie." It brought me great sadness because I made a direct correlation to the way others saw me and the way that I saw myself. If I could be compared to a drug addict, there was no room for beauty.

A ray of sunshine for me was academics. I excelled and always made good grades. I also played basketball and was successful, but still never seemed to escape the scrutiny of my skin color. Even my talent was not good enough to stop the comments. No matter how good I was, all anyone ever saw me as was "dark skinned."

Even my home life was a constant reminder of my skin color. My mother was a much lighter complexion. Most of my family members were lighter than I was, so I always felt out of place. My mother and father always told me that I was pretty, but it was never enough; I've always believed that all

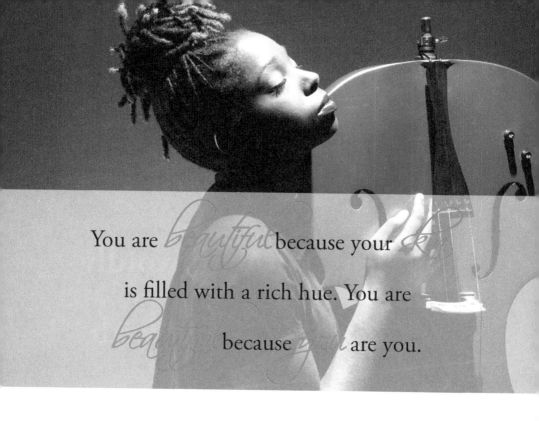

You are *beautiful* because your *skin* is filled with a rich hue. You are *beautiful* because *you* are you.

mothers and fathers think their children are beautiful, but I never believed that the world saw me as beautiful.

As time passed, the beautiful Hawaiian sun would add even more pigment to my complexion. The darker I got, the less beautiful I felt. In an act of desperation, I began to bleach my skin. I used bleaching creams for a period of six months but to no avail.

Although I have not yet fully accepted myself, I have discovered that I find great joy in making others laugh, and I am good at it. I can sing, play the piano, and am a good friend to others. I experience joy when I am able to bring joy to others. In these moments, I feel beautiful. My light is in bringing light to the world, and I know that my beautiful journey will keep allowing me to do so while I learn to love the reflection that I see in the mirror.

I want dark-skinned girls everywhere to know that there is no such thing as "cute to be dark skinned." You are beautiful because your skin is filled with a rich hue. You are beautiful because you are you.

I'm rich! Not with wordly *treasures* but with the priceless treasure of a beautiful *spirit* that withstands the test of time.

~ ARDRE ORIE

CONSCIOUSLY *Beautiful* THOUGHTS

TAYLOR

It is almost as though *we* have been conditioned to not *accept* our own beauty and, more sadly, covet the *beauty* of others.

*I*n my mind, the fact that we are different colors is a good thing.

I have never understood why people try to place a label on beauty or its characteristics. I am culturally strong and aware. My home life reflects constant exposure to African American literature, music, and art. In the midst of my consciousness about who I am and who I was born to become, I'm finding that the comments and opinions of others can cause us to question what we know to be true if we allow them to.

I was born with green eyes and I believe that they are beautiful, but this does not make me any less African American. My peers often ask, "What are you mixed with?" When I respond that I am African American, it is as though this is not a good enough answer. I can often hear them saying, "I wish that I had light eyes." This saddens me because we are all beautiful. Since when does having green eyes make you prettier than someone with brown eyes? It is almost as though we have been conditioned to not accept our own beauty and, more sadly, covet the beauty of others.

The media is always presenting different images of what defines beauty based on a particular standard. I sometimes have difficulties with other students because of how I look. My peers have an ingrained idea of what black beauty is. Some of my features, like my light skin, eye color, and hair texture and length, are attractive to them, while my hair color and full lips are sometimes critiqued as unattractive. I am often asked why I don't dye my hair light brown or blonde or get a perm, and often students refer to my lips as "big" or "fat," giving a negative connotation to their size. In my culture, some women do not

When I *look* in the mirror, I am proud
to be exactly who *I am*.

have naturally straight hair. Does that mean that I am less beautiful? There is nothing wrong with having nappy hair. There is nothing wrong with having straight hair.

My beautiful journey, fortified with a strong sense of self, has resulted in high self-esteem. It is my full belief that we should accept and love ourselves as we are. When I look in the mirror, I am proud to be exactly who I am. I love the fact that within my race, you can have two chocolate people create a butter baby. ☺

Whether others see it or appreciate it, the variety helps me to be proud of who I am. When I look into the mirror, I see the world and its people. It is proof that God has his hand in all things, including the creation of people.

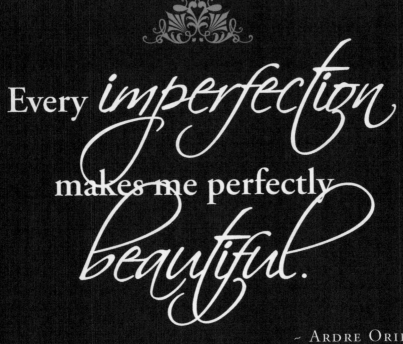

Every *imperfection*
makes me perfectly
beautiful.

~ ARDRE ORIE

CONSCIOUSLY *Beautiful* THOUGHTS

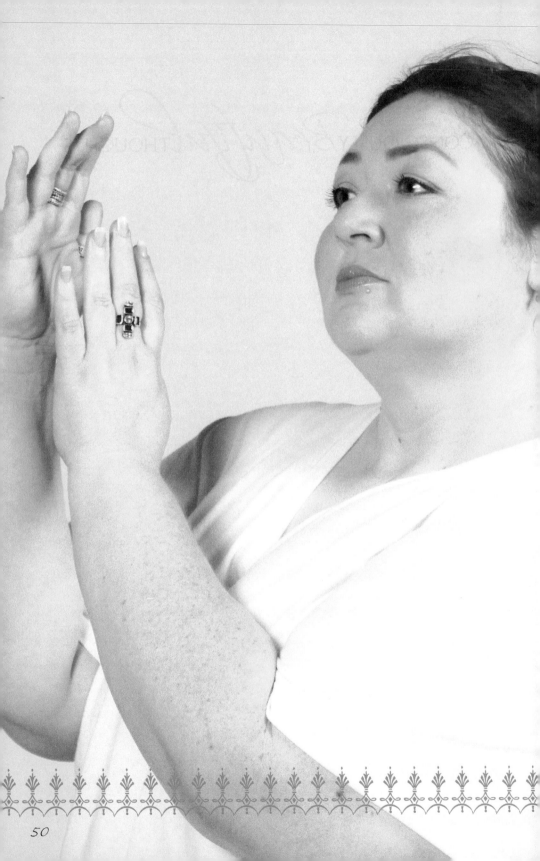

ADDIE

My *journey* was not about other people and what they *thought* of *me*, but more *importantly* what I thought about *myself*.

Beauty is all over me: the way I love, the way I see the world, and the way that I feel about myself. Growing up, I never dated because I thought that I wasn't good enough. The first real relationship that I got into resulted in systematic bouts of domestic violence. Things went from bad to worse when a fight ended with me having my leg broken for over six months.

I have always struggled with my weight, only to find out that I had complications with my thyroid. After having it removed, I lost 115 pounds, but I knew that I was destined to be a big girl. Most compliments that I received would often feel demeaning. People would say things like, "Addie, you have a really pretty face." I couldn't help but wonder: Did that mean that people didn't think the rest of me was pretty? From every angle—social media, magazines, and other news outlets—we are told that being big is not beautiful. There came a time in my life in which I resolved that I had to love myself. My journey was not about other people and what they thought of me, but more importantly what I thought about myself. No one was going to help me except me. I stayed in an abusive relationship because I thought it was the best that I could do. I was so wrong about so many things.

I decided that I loved me. When I fell in love with myself, I also found the love of my life. It's as though things have come full circle for me. I want to be an example for others to feel good about themselves. I have a niece watching and I would give anything to make sure that she knows how beautiful she is. I know that if she sees my confidence, she can have this same sense of self-love.

I am the most fabulous big girl in the room. I wear an invisible crown because I feel beautiful inside and out.

When I fell in *love* with *myself*, I also found the love of my *life*.

My fingerprint is all *my*

own as is my *beauty.*

~ ARDRE ORIE

CONSCIOUSLY *Beautiful* THOUGHTS

L

I do not regret my *journey* because it allowed me to bear witness to my *purpose* and walk in it every day that my light may *illuminate* a path for someone else.

Our ministries are birthed out of our experiences. I believe that giving birth to your ministry and giving birth to your purpose are synonymous.

God has spoken to me for as long as I remember. It still amazes me how abundantly he blessed me with gifts and talents for his purpose, but the path towards understanding their use was unclear and painful. I was adopted by my birth mother's best friend. My beautiful journey began with me believing that my birth mother had abandoned me. Like many women, I learned early in life how to mask pain, hurt, and fear.

Growing up, I remember witnessing my adopted father victimize my adopted mother with violence. On one occasion, the violence was so tremendous that, as I was standing in the doorway, he shoved me out of the room and slammed the door. In the bathroom, I distinctly remember planning to take the metal towel bar down to help my mother by returning his violence. My mother would later leave him, and we began a new life.

Around the age of six, we relocated to a smaller apartment. My journey became dark and would reveal several occurrences of molestation. The first time I was molested was by a family friend, and I was made to perform oral sex on him. The second occurrence of molestation happened at the hands of one of my mother's boyfriends. My mother was going to night school to better herself and did what we then referred to as "day's work." I remember distinctly the first time he came into my room and wished to block out the painful memories that no child should have to endure

As time went on and the molestation continued, he would give me money to not say anything. I was a child and looked to the adults in my life to teach and guide me as to right and wrong. At the time, this was the only place that I received the positive attention that we all seek, so I began to accept these acts as my truth. Often, he would take me to his home and give me snacks and many things that children adore. He also introduced me to the spirit of pornography as he would play it while engaging in inappropriate acts with me. I can still see the old black and white TV. Many other details I learned to block out, and I would make myself forget about each incident shortly after it happened. I had learned two things: (1) This act, sex, was a way to get attention and (2) I had something valuable that other people wanted. This would later paint the scenery for where my beautiful journey would evolve.

As I grew older, I sought comfort through sex. It was one of the few acts of affection that I knew. It was in the midst of that act that people would hug you and tell you that you were loved. That is what we all seek, to be loved.

At age 16, I was pregnant with my daughter, and at age 17, I was pregnant with my son. The father of my son wanted to keep our family together and asked me to move in with him. He was planning to leave for college and had done well in receiving scholarships for his education. Due to my lack of exposure, I was completely uncomfortable with moving, growing, and expanding my horizons, so I declined.

I did, however, visit and remember thinking that the college campus represented a new world. There was more to life than what I had experienced, but fear held me hostage to my circumstance.

As time went on, my adopted mother became licensed to be an Evangelist. When she got saved, our lives changed significantly.

I became what I feel was the typical PK. I began going to teen clubs, and my passion for dancing emerged. I was absolutely intrigued by my love for ballet.

Unlike most who wanted to drink and do drugs, I attended the clubs to dance. I could often be seen with a bottle of water while on the dance floor. I was in dance crews, talent shows, etc. I became involved in theatre, dancing, and performing.

At age 27, I was hired to perform at a dinner theatre. I thought that it was the start of my ability to create a true life for myself and my family. I bought a car and moved into my own apartment. Shortly after moving in the right direction, I would receive news of a detour. The dinner theatre was preparing to close.

Relentlessly, I began to search for jobs that could fit my skill set. Through a routine search in the classifieds, I saw an ad for dancing five days a week. The ad boasted that the dancers could earn "thousands per week." Auditions were being held at 9:30 p.m., which was of no shock value to me because this was also the time that my previous dinner theatre would host auditions.

When I arrived for the audition, I was more than shocked as I realized that the search had led me to an exotic dancing club. I decided to go inside for the audition but knew that I would not be hired because I had no prior experience in this type of setting. To my surprise, I was hired on the spot, and they instructed me to begin working immediately. After four hours of work, I had cleared $600. With my car payment, rent, and, most importantly, my family on my mind, I knew that this new profession would become an intricate part of my beautiful journey.

Within a four month span, I went from rarely consuming alcohol to a becoming an alcoholic and a drug abuser. I began taking cocaine, acid, ecstasy, and ketamine just to get by. In the midst of this type of lifestyle, sober was the last state of being that I wanted to be in. I could not believe that my life had turned on such a path; I had witnessed a drug addicted family member and distinctly remember thinking how much I did not want that direction for my life. But even in the midst of this turmoil, the voice of God never departed from my spirit.

Even in the dressing rooms of the strip club, I would pray with the girls, read my Bible, and minister to the other dancers, often at their request. What stood out to me most was that others could still see that I had a relationship with God, in the midst of some of my darkest moments.

The darkness would turn to light when I realized that I no longer wanted to be in this lifestyle. On a particular night, a guy friend of mine decided that he was going to drive me to work, wait for me to get off, and drive me back home. Prior to this evening, I got high before going in to work and always had cocktails to go to sleep at night, but this night was different. I did not get high or drunk for work; I was completely sober. As the night progressed, our club was raided. The laws in our state mandated that any sexual acts in exchange for money were deemed prostitution. This meant that everyone in our club was guilty.

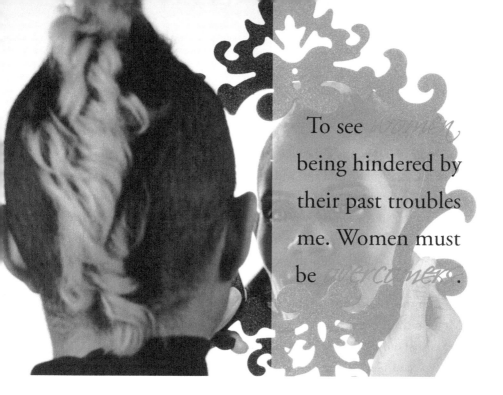

To see women being hindered by their past troubles me. Women must be overcomers.

In the midst of the raid, there was complete chaos. The lights came on and I watched as girls were being escorted out in handcuffs one by one, and I knew that I would be next. I knew that night that I would go to jail for prostitution.

I was seated in a booth in the club that was extremely dim, so even when the lights came on, I was not immediately discovered. I sat up to observe the confusion, and in the middle of the dance floor, I saw an officer who appeared to be illuminated. He spoke words that my ears heard with a resounding roar, but I distinctly remember that his mouth never moved. I heard him say, "Get your things and leave."

The next moment was like a scene from a movie. It was as if someone had pressed the pause button. Everything was still; there was no movement, no

sound, and no chaos. I retreated to the dressing room, grabbed my things, and began walking towards the door. I looked back, and the officer was still illuminated, still with eyes on me. I stepped across the threshold of the club into the foyer, and it was as if the pause was released and the chaos reinstated.

That night, I went home and had the best night of sleep that I had ever experienced in my entire life. I didn't drink to go to sleep as I had normally done. When I awoke, I did not wish for the usual cocktail that was required for me to wake up. I began to ransack my home, emptying every bottle of alcohol that I could find, and I threw away all of the drugs; I no longer had a use for either. I was delivered from my addiction of drugs and alcohol overnight. From that night forward, I never danced in that capacity again.

My beautiful journey would take me back to the church and a life of seeking Christ only. After a great deal of searching and fasting, I would later hear the voice of God tell me to return to the very club that I had been delivered from. In retrospect, my purpose for returning wasn't much different than before; I just wore a different hat. I returned to minister with the girls and pray with them. It is not normal for people to be permitted to go in the dressing rooms with the dancers for safety and privacy. I was welcomed with open arms. Some people recognized me and some did not, but my mission was clear. God would later reveal to me that the only way I could have ever gotten inside was to be an insider. This was powerful.

Today, my gifts and talents have led me to a life of fashion designing and liturgical dancing for his glory. I now spend my days creating couture fashions for my clothing line The Dare Collection, which empowers women to clothe their bodies, and, with my company Temples Dance, LLC, I teach children how to avoid the pressure to dance like the images portrayed in mainstream media and how to use their bodies to express themselves in respectful ways.

We all have a different road that we travel, but it is still a road. We may not be going in the same direction, but we will all end up in the same space. To see women being hindered by their past troubles me. Women must be overcomers.

I am now free. I do not regret my journey because it allowed me to bear witness to my purpose and walk in it every day that my light may illuminate a path for someone else. No abuse, whether self-inflicted or caused by the hands of others, can keep you from your divine purpose. If you have breath, you have purpose.

I believe in my beauty.

I am enough.

~ ARDRE ORIE

CONSCIOUSLY *Beautiful* THOUGHTS

ANNA

When you *dance* to the beat of

your own drum, you often find

the *essence* of your *heart*.

When you dance to the beat of your own drum, you often find the essence of your heart. We do not exist to be like anyone else, for we are as vast as fingerprints. I myself am multi-talented. For many years, I was a Special Olympics gymnast and a Global Messenger for the Special Olympics. I spent a great deal of my time giving speeches to organizations to create awareness about the Special Olympics. The world should know that being different means being amazing! I love myself, and I always feel pretty.

In addition to being a gymnast, I am an amazing dancer, and I perform for packed crowds at my recital every spring. I participate in the Habima Theatre Group with the Marcus Jewish Community Center in Atlanta. Our group is a theatrical organization filled with professional adult actors, including some with disabilities. I've performed in Once Upon A Mattress, Footloose, Happy Days, and Grease, just to name a few. I love to express myself through dance because it makes me feel beautiful. I always feel beautiful because my family tells me I am.

If I could tell women and girls one thing, it is to be true to yourself and learn to express yourself.

One day I would love to do fashion modeling because when I look in the mirror, I see a princess who likes to rock out! Until then, I am in love with just being me.

If I could tell *women* and *girls* one thing, it is to be *true to* yourself and learn to *express yourself*.

I *make* no apologies
for what I have come to
recognize as *beautiful.*
Take me as I am or watch me
as I *walk* away.

~ ARDRE ORIE

CONSCIOUSLY *Beautiful* THOUGHTS

D I N A

The *love* and support of my *family*

helps me to appreciate my *journey*

because I know that I am *unique*.

*I*f you ask me, normal is overrated. We spend so much time trying to be like other people that we can often forget how amazing we really are.

My beautiful journey began with my mom, who is 100% Greek, and my dad, who is Italian and German. I consider myself white/European, and like every other teen on a quest to love the reflection in the mirror, there have been times that I did not feel pretty. I can honestly say that I still have those moments.

The love and support of my family helps me to appreciate my journey because I know that I am unique. It makes me feel so much better knowing that I have a supportive family who encourages me and helps me recognize my beauty.

Both my mom and step-dad help me to build my self-confidence and boy do I listen.

In the past years, while I was in public school, my schoolmates were kind of mean to me. They would make comments because I did not feel pressured to wear any make-up. I was affected negatively because I really wanted to fit in.

There are times when I read magazines, and the message seems to be that we are only beautiful when we are as thin as sticks, as blonde as possible, and wearing way more than enough makeup. I do not agree. You do not need to be a rodeo clown to be beautiful. When I begin to make comparisons between myself and the magazines, my mother always reminds me that what I see is merely a perfect picture. I know that no person is without their own personal challenges, and I continue to be encouraged along my beautiful journey.

Although I have never aspired to be a model, I do enjoy being photographed, and I am finding my way towards being comfortable just the way that I am.

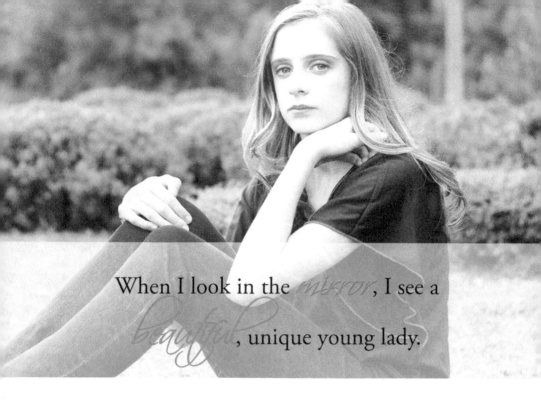

When I look in the *mirror*, I see a *beautiful*, unique young lady.

I have learned that the true picture of a person is what is inside, their emotions, their fears and their problems. I want girls to know that we should all be exactly who we are and forget all of the messages that we receive from others. You do not need to be 50 pounds to be pretty. You do not need to cake on the make-up and dress a certain way to fit in. Be yourself, be unique, and have your own style, even if it's weird. At least in the end, you will be unique and different, which is perfect.

When I look in the mirror, I see a beautiful, unique young lady. Sure, I am not perfect, but who cares.

I want to be remembered as a person who makes a difference in the world even though I am not perfect. I want to show the world that you do not have to be "beautiful" in the world's sense of the word to make a difference. I just want people to appreciate themselves exactly the way they are.

My *beauty* is a subtle secret but the *love* in my *heart* roars.

~ ARDRE ORIE

CONSCIOUSLY *Beautiful* THOUGHTS

MALIAKA

I did not want to be different.

Every freckle on my face tells a beautiful story of culture, ancestry, and triumph. My mother was born in St. Thomas, Virgin Islands, and my freckles were inherited from her French Creole father. My father, who is African American, was born in Hopewell, VA. According to the U.S. Census Bureau, my race is Black Caribbean. I was raised primarily by my father. This factor and my race would be the beginning point of my beautiful journey. At the age of four, my parents officially divorced and my father remarried to a woman of black and Mexican decent. My siblings and I were cared for by a live-in nanny, a woman from Mexico.

At a young age, my freckles began to appear. I can still hear the voices of curious children asking me: "What's wrong with your face?" "What is that on your face?" "Why do you have dots on your face?" It was during this period that I began to wonder why I looked different. At this point, I felt sad about my beauty. I was different. Different to me meant strange, weird, and uncomfortable.

With my father's job, my family relocated to Midland, TX. This stop in my beautiful journey would prove to be more challenging as I noticed that Spanish-speaking children were not favored. I determined that I would no longer speak in Spanish and lived life without acknowledging this part of my culture. I did not want to be different. Quickly, I lost my Spanish-speaking skills. Even so, my freckles were a constant reminder of my mother's face.

Life continued to high school, and I remember attending a school in which the rebel flag flew proudly. On one occasion, an African American female teenager approached me in an angry rage and screamed, "I will slap the freckles off your face, my boyfriend doesn't like you...!" I was in such shock that I wet my pants in fright. I never had any association with the young man that she spoke of. I gleaned that I had to do something to erase the freckles that continued to cause me so much pain and despair. In desperation, I stopped eating lunch and saved my lunch money to purchase bleaching cream from the local drug store. I applied the bleaching cream daily, but the freckles remained.

My first boyfriend in high school was white. One time, he took me home to meet his parents, and at first glance, he was told that his truck would be taken from him if he continued to see me. It was at that moment that my naturally curly hair surpassed my status as an honor student with a 4.4 GPA, the highest of any black female in my graduating class. My freckles surpassed the fact that I was an engineer assistant for Mobil Oil or that I was offered four college scholarships. I was simply heartbroken that my physical attributes meant more than the excellence that I had achieve in academia.

I soon realized that
prejudice will
always exist, although
it's only *powerful*
when I allow
myself to be
defined by it.

From that day forward, I made a decision to not wear my hair curly again. People seemed more comfortable around me when my hair was straight. The more I looked like those around me, the more people seemed to like me.

In high school, my dreams of becoming an actress were deferred when my drama director told me that I would be unable to maintain a lead role as the wife of a white actor. My roles were reduced from lead roles to assisting roles due to my race. I was told that society would not be accepting of my participation in such a role. I became discouraged with pursuing a career as an actor, and as an adult I became a teacher instead.

In retrospect, I feel as if I allowed society to define me.

I never stopped my pursuit of excellence and went on to attend a university in the Dallas, TX, area in hopes of escaping small town prejudices. I soon realized that prejudice will always exist, although it's only powerful when I allow myself to be defined by it. I went on to discover love and marry a man of fair complexion from Costa Rica. I felt tremendous joy when my child was born with lighter skin as I felt that he would have a better chance at life and a better journey than mine. Upon divorcing and becoming a single parent, I was told by a male I dated, "I wouldn't want a child by you, because I would not want my child to have freckles." My beautiful journey of not being accepted by others seemed to be reality more than perception.

In addition to my freckles and complexion, I also found myself working harder to be respected with a large chest. I worked hard to cover myself and feel confident but nothing seemed to work.

My beautiful journey up until this point had been filled with heartache and pain, but was absent of triumph. To help myself work through the pain, I attended a counseling session and was told that I suffered from low self-esteem.

These words upset me because I was in denial. I never returned to counseling.

One day I got sick and tired of being sick and tired and began to work on myself.

I learned through self-help books and textbooks from my bachelor's degree in psychology that it is important for me to love myself and remain confident. Reading the Bible and black history books also helped me to discover my true worth.

As I have matured and grown older, I flaunt and work with what I have confidently. I'm seeing clearly now and know beauty comes from within. No matter how much someone loves me, I have to depend on myself, my own

thoughts and actions, to reach maximum success. I have learned to not let what others think of me change how I think about myself.

Besides my son, my proudest moment came when I walked across the stage to obtain my master's degree with a perfect 4.0 GPA. I was the first of my entire family generation to obtain a master's degree. My parents awarded me with a financial gift and a two-week trip to Mexico to participate in a Spanish language class. Today, I enjoy my career in education, but one day after I retire, I may fulfill that dream of becoming an actress because society cannot and will not define me or determine what is beautiful! What does God say? I believe he says my freckles are uncountable kiss marks from him. He made me unique and perfectly designed! I love my unique beauty! I love me! I'm Consciously Beautiful!

ALDA

There was room for me to *work harder* to be a *good person* and do the very best in life with the *opportunities* that I was *given.*

I can honestly say that I never really owned my pretty. My beautiful journey began in a single-parent home with a mother who stood tall at 6'4, with drive, determination, and fearlessness to match. Although I have only seen my father twice in my entire life, my mother taught me that everything in life had to be earned. From this disposition, I coveted my academic performance. I was confident in my ability to do well and I succeeded. I never really focused on outer beauty, although I recognized that I was always much

taller than my peers. My friends scrutinized me and would often accuse me of "thinking that I was white" because academics was of the upmost importance to me. This focus, although criticized by many, helped me to travel confidently along my beautiful journey. Even though I was taller than everyone else, I witnessed my mother wear heels confidently. She laid a foundation for me to not only accept but own my height.

In retrospect, I realized that although introverted, I never really gave people all of me because I did not want to conform to or be encapsulated by the expectations of others. By the time I reached college, I decided to just be me.

I don't have to live up to everyone else's expectations of me. I've learned that misfortune can lead to triumph. I've learned that I was in control of what I thought about myself, and for everything that I did not have control over, such as not having my father in my life, there was room for me to work harder to be a good person and do the very best in life with the opportunities that I was given.

As long as God is happy with me, then that is all that matters.

Today, I give people who I really am. I am 6'0 tall. I am smart. I am classy, and I love the reflection that I see in the mirror.

As long as *God* is happy with
me, then that is all that *matters*.

I've always known that
revealing meant *sharing*
a little of my beauty at
a *time* as opposed to
giving it all away and
leaving nothing for the
imagination.

~ ARDRE ORIE

CONSCIOUSLY *Beautiful* THOUGHTS

MACHELLE

There will *always* be someone who

does not like something about you,

but it does not make *you* any less.

Awkward. Insecure. Alone. These are the best words that I can use to describe the start of my beautiful journey. My road was rocky to say the least. I always felt that I stood out like a sore thumb. I was always the tallest. I had orange hair, freckles, and huge glasses. At just ten years old, I wore a size D-cup bra. As a teenager, I worked so hard to be loyal to my friends because I never felt a complete sense of stability at home. I would later learn that even friends can't fill every void.

I never felt good enough for anything. Most people find at least one thing that they like or enjoy, but my low self-esteem would not allow me to do so.

At age 12, I felt suicidal and my beautiful journey arrived at a stop sign. I had to make a decision to go either left or right. On the left, my friends were doing drugs, having sex, and abusing alcohol. On the right, there were a few friends who were grounded in their religion. I observed the outcomes of those on the left and opted to make a right turn. I tried God.

I found great comfort in religion and would often read the Bible. Although I did not know what I was reading, I knew that there was a higher power that I could depend on. When I found God, I felt like I had found a father. I got baptized and continued to teach myself to pray by talking to God in the same way that I imagined talking to my father.

As time passed, my relationship with God continued to grow, but my self-esteem stood still in time. I remember never being anybody's choice. A guy that I really liked and admired told me that he had something to tell me, and to my excitement, I thought that he might also share in my sentiment for him. He went on to tell me, "You're like a guy's best friend. You are better than a dog." Although he later told me that he just meant that I was an amazing friend, his words shaped how I thought of myself and how I believed guys saw me.

I was lucky to not have engaged in pre-marital sex and many of the other behaviors that low self-esteem can often lead to on our beautiful journeys.

With my faith in God, I decided to take a brave leap of faith and leave home the day before my 17th birthday. I will never forget my foster mother asking me what kind of cake that I would like for my birthday. Her actions reminded me of love. I told her that I really liked sunflowers, and the next day, my 17th birthday, she presented me with a cake wrapped in two artificial sunflowers. These sunflowers symbolize love, and to this day, they are the first decoration that I place in my home.

At age 19, I was discovered by a modeling agency. I had never worn heels, makeup, or walked on a runway. I was not even sure if I believed what they thought of me. They thought that I was beautiful, but I still saw the awkward girl with huge glasses in the mirror. I've always seen myself as the "strong one," not the "pretty one."

I have learned to be *proud* of exactly who *I am* and accept the things that I cannot *change*.

After getting married, I became a proud mother. The weight gain of motherhood took a toll on me as well. I took the mirrors down in the bathroom because I could not stand to see myself get out of the shower.

Today, I am a work in progress. When I am in front of the camera, I believe that I am what others see, and I work to embody this same confidence during my day-to-day experiences. I work extremely hard to teach my children to love the reflection that they see in the mirror. In my home, we do not speak of diets and only discuss healthy eating habits and embracing what we have been given.

I know now that I was chasing acceptance from society, which can often lead to a dead end.

There will always be someone who does not like something about you, but it does not make you any less. Although I still have to work to maintain my self-esteem, I have learned to be proud of exactly who I am and accept the things that I cannot change.

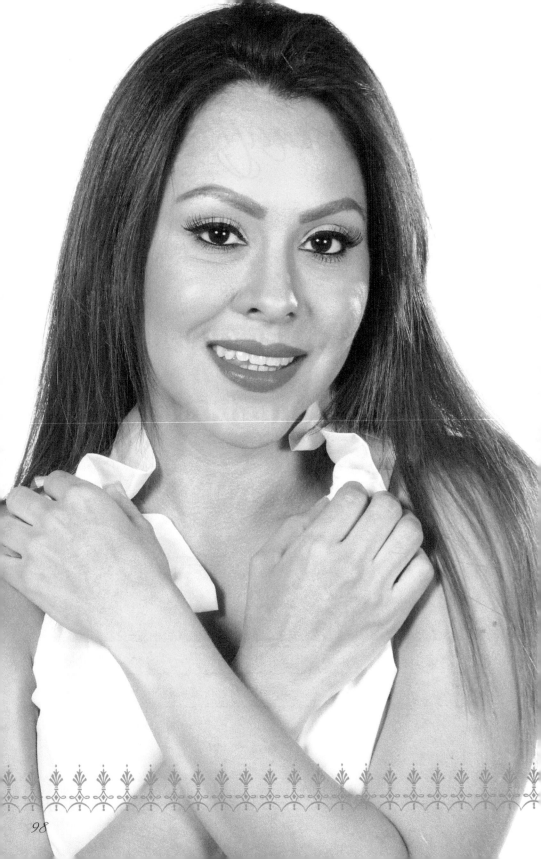

LETY

All women and girls *deserve*

to know that they are the greatest

miracles of nature.

I've never felt anything other than beautiful. While growing up in Mexico, both my mother and father always whispered softly telling me that I was beautiful. Their whispers eventually turned into the GPS that would guide me along my beautiful journey. It is because of them that I have been able to maintain a love of self. More importantly, they showed me through constant love and sacrifice that family means everything.

At the age of 16, I relocated to the United States and immediately began working. I learned the power of being self-sufficient. Now I felt beautiful and

powerful. I bought my first car brand new because of my ability to maintain employment. I became driven and, with the support of my family, continued to thrive. The only component missing was love.

When I did find It, I loved hard and I lost. My relationships would result in possessive and even abusive behaviors, and I knew they would never work. Although now divorced and mother to two beautiful sons, I have no regrets. My beautiful journey has taught me to trust my instincts and never devalue the woman I see in the mirror. I am not in search of love because I found the greatest love inside of me. I have never felt that I need another person to complete me, and I owe my strength to the confidence that my parents instilled in me long ago.

All women and girls deserve to know that they are the greatest miracles of nature. I want women and girls to know that there will never be another with your mind, your heart, your eyes, your hands. No one can walk, talk, or, most importantly, think exactly like you. You are unique, and that is why you are beautiful.

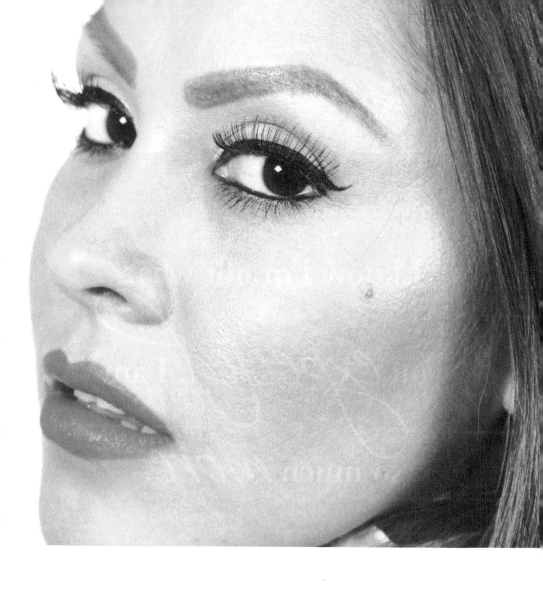

You are *unique*, and that is
why you are *beautiful*.

NATALIE

The *color* of my skin is what makes me who *I am*!

believe that God is an artist, who loves colors, sizes, shapes, and textures.

I've never really thought of myself as beautiful; I just enjoy being me. My Russian heritage and freckled face distinguish me.

My beautiful journey began around the age of three when I looked in the mirror and noticed my freckles. I asked my mother if they were contagious and if I was the only one who had them. I wondered if they would ever go away.

My mother went on to tell me that I had been kissed by angels, and I have felt proud of exactly who I am ever since.

At a young age, I auditioned for a national talent search for acting, and was encouraged by the scouts to consider modeling. I know that my alabaster skin makes me unique.

We live in a society that teaches us that tanned skin is healthy, and often people ask me if I am feeling okay because I am pale. I have never had a tan because my skin is very sensitive to the sun and I burn very easily. I have no desire to use tanning lotions or any other extreme measures to change the color of my skin.

The color of my skin is what makes me who I am!

I have been influenced by my family to know that remaining focused on helping others and less on myself would build a solid foundation for my self-esteem.

Most importantly, education is a top priority in our house, which steers me in the right direction along my beautiful journey.

Three things that I know for sure:

1. We are all uniquely and beautifully made in his image.

2. There are no two people on this planet that are exactly the same.

3. We must learn to embrace and love the person that we see in the mirror.

The next chapter in my beautiful journey will include me going to college and becoming an attorney. When I look in the mirror, I see a girl with a very bright future ahead of her!

When I *look* in the mirror, I see

a girl with a very *bright future*

ahead of her!

Well don't just stand there. Go ahead, tell me *I'm beautiful.* I'll be sure to tell you that I'm *smart.* That's what I want you to remember about *me.*

~ ARDRE ORIE

108

CONSCIOUSLY *Beautiful* THOUGHTS

SHANA

I was motivated to *love* every part of *me.*

I was no longer afraid to tell the world,

"This is who I am."

Statuesque is not the main ingredient in the recipe for being beautiful. Rather, the most important element is the love of self. I was raised by both my mother and father in an amazing family filled with love that left me with only fond memories of childhood. My journey towards feeling beautiful met its first challenges when I turned 17. I began to experience tremendous acne that would leave very noticeable scars on my face. I tried to experiment with makeup and found myself most empowered when I researched ways to take better care of my skin. Along my beautiful journey, I found myself refusing to smile with my teeth showing because my beauty revealed a gap.

As an aspiring model, I began to study beautiful ladies walking the runway, and to my surprise, a few of those beautiful faces had gaps in their front teeth. These ladies were confident with their look and I realized that I could be too. I was motivated to love every part of me. I was no longer afraid to tell the world, "This is who I am."

I'm confident with who I am, from the way I walk and talk to the kindness of my heart. It might sound cliché' but I was raised in a loving home in which my parents provided a healthy platform for my self-esteem and as an adult, I still feel good about myself today. You do not have to arrive at the destination of self-love and self-acceptance from pain. It is possible to love yourself in the midst of happiness as well.

Today, when I look in the mirror, I see a beautiful young woman staring back at me who is still learning something new each day! People sometimes forget that beauty shines from within.

My journey has proven to me that knowledge is power. At each fork in the road, I arm myself with information about the areas in which I have questions. I now know that I am one of a kind and I am not meant to look like everyone else.

I now know that I am *one of a kind* and I am not meant to look like everyone else.

You have no idea what pain
I have been through. My
beauty pierces your soul
like the stars pierce the sky.
It is because of my *story*
that I am indeed beautiful.

~ ARDRE ORIE

CONSCIOUSLY *Beautiful* THOUGHTS

LISA

As an adult, I've learned that my *beauty* is *unique* because it defines *me!*

I am Cherokee Indian. As a child and teenager, there were many times I didn't feel pretty, inside or out. There was and continues to be so much peer pressure from others, but my family has always been supportive in whatever I've done in my life. As an adult, I've learned that my beauty is unique because it defines me!

My beautiful journey began in the entertainment business. For as long as I can remember, I have been performing, and at age five, I hit the big stage. These experiences were the starting point for who I believed myself to be.

I recall a sense of urgency to be perfect in the eyes of managers, agents, and photographers. I wanted the industry to love me; it can place a great

deal of pressure on you to look and behave in specified ways. My beautiful journey would eventually guide me to a sign that read: "Perfect People Aren't Real and Real People Aren't Perfect."

I can still hear those whispers of the industry that told me that I was too short, or that my thighs were too thick. I was even told that my nose was not big enough. No matter how strong you are, words can and do hurt. Like many women, I struggled to stay the course and not veer off the road towards low self-esteem. That has been my greatest struggle. My personal definition of self-esteem is how much you feel you are worth and how much you feel that other people value you. I feel that our self-esteem is so important because it affects our mental health.

I have learned to surround myself with a support system that helps me stay the course. I understand the importance of having positive people in your life. My family is tremendously supportive of me, and my core group of friends keep positivity flowing. Furthermore, I have grown to understand that my attitude makes all the difference. If I maintain a positive attitude, my outlook on life is positive, and I am empowered to enjoy all that life has to offer.

Like most, I do compare myself to models and images that I see in the media. It's hard not to. But my body is my own, no matter what shape or size I am. I am learning to embrace me for who I am, not who I think I need to be. I have always longed to be perfect, and I am learning how to accept my imperfections. We all have them, and we must all learn to love them. They are what make us unique.

My beautiful journey today is very much the same as it has been, although I travel with more wisdom, courage, and acceptance of myself.

I continue to work in the industry, and I am privileged to be an extra in several films.

No one can or should *love* me more than *me*.

I am still working to love the reflection that I see in the mirror. I know that I am loved, and this speaks great volumes to my self-esteem. I now must learn to be 100% happy with who I am. No one can or should love me more than me.

My beautiful journey has also taught me that we should strive to be a positive light for others. I want my light to radiate as a shining example for my daughter, so that she might realize that beauty is about how you live your life, the choices you make, and the people you help. How we carry ourselves is what truly defines who we are.

We must all remember that we will be defined by the dash between the date we were born and the date that we depart this earth.

What we made others feel will long surpass what they saw with their eyes.

To all the ladies who question their *beauty* because of what society says, I say we question society for making us *believe* that the reflection in the mirror wasn't *good* enough.

~ ARDRE ORIE

CONSCIOUSLY *Beautiful* THOUGHTS

CONSCIOUSLY BEAUTIFUL

TREASURE

I am *comfortable* being a
mixed race black woman. I am
authentic, and I no longer
feel inferior to my own people.

There are times when our journey for self-acceptance is a road filled with spirals, twists, and turns. My road was just that. I recall a time when I went to school and a dark-skinned girl attempted to pull my ponytails off my head because she said that she wanted her hair to be like mine. Marred by confusion, I have always hated my hair, and in the midst of that experience, I thought that I could potentially dislike dark-skinned girls as well. Sometimes being different means standing out. I worked hard to be more "down," more "cool," a little more "edgy" to mirror my environment. I realized in later years that I was only in search of acceptance.

Born in Atlanta, Georgia, I am Columbian and African American and the oldest of three siblings. I am the only sibling with a Columbian heritage. For this and other reasons, complexion has always been a topic of discussion. I often witnessed my mother bear the burden of the search for self-love, and I can only imagine that much of my disposition was initiated in observation. My mother would bleach her skin which further solidified the fact that our skin was not beautiful.

When I was born, my mother did not have an instant connection with me. She did not wish to hold my hand out in public, and we struggled to find the instant mother–daughter bond that some feel. I can hear my mother saying, "When you go to school, some girls will not like you." At the time, I did not understand why. She was, however, correct. I did not relate to my classmates, and no one seemed to relate to me. Due to my mixed heritage, I did not look like my classmates, nor did they resemble me. I spoke differently and did not maintain any of the same interests as most. I found love and joy in writing.

I was teased, bullied, and picked on. I developed a resentment for dark-skinned girls; they became the enemy. They hated me, and I could not find the love for myself in the midst of the chaos.

We must be comfortable in our own skin, *love ourselves*, and respect ourselves, so others will respect us.

In high school, I was awkward. I was tall, slim, and flat-chested, and I had a gap in my teeth. Guys did not like me and would even refer to my gap as a "prison bar." I was called "raccoon," and I maintained very poor posture because I was insecure. It is amazing what your posture can reveal about you.

Although it took me a long time to be comfortable with who I am, I look in the mirror today and I see beauty. I recognize that I don't have to change who I am to meet a standard that someone else has set.

I am comfortable being a mixed-race black woman. I am authentic, and I no longer feel inferior to my own people.

We must be comfortable in our own skin, love ourselves, and respect ourselves, so others will respect us.

Beauty is and should always be on *purpose.*

~ Ardre Orie

CONSCIOUSLY *Beautiful* THOUGHTS

NELISSHA

I am learning how to appreciate my *unique*

beauty and appreciate the fact that

I don't *look* like anyone else.

*S*ometimes in silence, there are screams for help. Sometimes in silence there is pain.

I have never been a loud or boisterous person and spent a great deal of my childhood observing as opposed to speaking. When I was born I was very fair in complexion and had very large lips, both of which I did not love or appreciate. I was much lighter than both of my parents and often attributed this as the reason that my father left. At the age of 11 my father returned and we began to rebuild the pieces of our family. These factors would later create the backdrop to my beautiful journey.

At the age of seven, I developed an affinity for ice skating after watching Michelle Kwan on TV. After skating for nearly seven years, I knew without

question that I was beautiful when I skated. These moments of freedom were intricate details along my beautiful journey.

In high school, a time where most girls are doing everything possible to be noticed and paid attention to, I had one goal: to go unnoticed, to be unseen, to be invisible. You've seen the girl that was as quiet as a mouse, never speaking, laughing, or engaging much with others. She was the one that never raised her hand or made many friends. That girl was me. I appeared to be quiet, shy, and reserved. Some might call it introverted. Most failed to realize that my silence masked great pain. I was not seen, nor heard, and always walked with my head down.

I always felt as though I did not belong in my home environment as well as my social environment. I liked different music and my interests were totally different from my family and those who could be potential friends. I felt like there was no place for me.

I would later learn that I possessed such a deep sense of feeling that, often, I avoided my feelings altogether. I am compassionate in a way that most people could never understand, and this led me to remain in silence.

After moving to Germany with my father's job, I saw a ray of hope because I was able to experience true friendship. My newly found BFF helped me to laugh, and I found beauty in laughter.

I felt like I was suffocating when we returned to the U.S. as my father's job required us to relocate again.

I began to suffer from anxiety and often felt like I did not want to live. To hurt myself, I would overeat. This was something that I could control.

I had an epiphany and realized a very important factor: Things were not getting better for me because deep inside, I did not want help.

But I also realized that I did not want to spend the rest of my life as an outsider or feeling as though I did not belong. I realized that I had to first be willing to accept myself before I could ever expect anyone else to accept me.

I must *love* the
reflection that I
see in the mirror;
she *deserves* it.

I have learned to seek information and read a lot of self-help books. I also began counseling and was placed on medication. For me, this has helped. It has helped me to talk to someone that I did not know.

Now, when I look in the mirror there are times when I love my beauty, and on other occasions, I avoid mirrors all together. I am learning how to appreciate my unique beauty and appreciate the fact that I don't look like anyone else.

I am learning that I must love me first. I must understand myself first. I must accept myself before I can ask anyone else to do so. I must love the reflection that I see in the mirror; she deserves it.

You won't forget my *face,*
it tells a *beautiful* story.

~ ARDRE ORIE

CONSCIOUSLY *Beautiful* THOUGHTS

FULL CIRCLE

I can honestly say that my beautiful journey continues to evolve. Now, well into my 30's, I am comfortable in my own skin. I believe this to be the result of life's experiences, consistent prayer, and a constant quest to be a better human being.

Through the course of writing this book, my father departed this life. It was in his death that I was released from the bondage that I had allowed myself to be a victim to for so long. During his service, I bore witness to pictures of myself as well as my family (my children and husband) that he held so dearly. I would later learn that he loved me. In this moment of realization, I was accepted. For so long I walked my beautiful journey blindly, feeling that there must have been something wrong with me that he left me as a child, that he did not love me, that I was not enough. My father loved me in his way, and although he no longer walks on this side, my love for him has grown immensely because I accept that he loved the way that he knew how. I also accepted responsibility for the hurt that I caused myself. Although hard to admit, I chose to be oppressed by the notion that I was not enough. I could have chosen the latter. We must choose the life, love, and sentiments that we want to be the resounding themes for our lives and not allow another human to hold the key to unlocking our happiness. We are each responsible for the way we feel, think, and speak of ourselves.

With a new found freedom, I am convinced now more than ever that I must do all that I can to make a difference and assist women and girls in the process of discovering the love of self. I find that I feel most beautiful when I am in the midst of helping others. These acts remove the importance of my attire, disposition in society, financial status, and, most importantly, my appearance. Acts of kindness make me see the world and my reason for existence differently. This book is the ultimate embodiment of that.

It is my mission to reach as many women and girls as humanly possible to share this message. To ensure this end, I have established the Consciously

Beautiful Movement, an active extension of the book. The Consciously Beautiful Movement exists to empower women and girls to love the reflection they see in the mirror and demystify and deconstruct media messages that demean women and girls.

The *Consciously Beautiful Movement* hosts the following activities annually to empower women and girls in the U.S. and beyond:

CB BOOK TALK TOUR

Multi-city tour with author Ardre Orie sharing the messages of triumph and self-discovery with intimate groups of readers and audiences.

CB EMPOWERMENT SESSIONS

The focus for all CB Empowerment Sessions is teaching women and girls to recognize and demystify harmful media messages and inaccurate portrayals that degrade the value of women and girls. Attendees leave with an increased awareness of media tactics and strategies to filter messages for self-sustainability.

CB MENTAL HEALTH CONSORTIUM

The CB Mental Health Consortium is a network of mental health professionals and resources that assist in the provision of women's and girls' use and knowledge of effective strategies to increase self-acceptance and maintain healthy lifestyle practices to thrive.

CB ANNUAL HEART 2 HEART RETREAT

The CB Annual Heart 2 Heart Retreat encourages openness and authenticity and allows women to engage in activities to acknowledge, understand, and love the reflection that they see in the mirror.

PINK WISH ACADEMY

In partnership with the Pink Wish Foundation (www.pinkwishfoundation. org), Consciously Beautiful in Pink offers self-esteem building programs for schools, church groups, and local community groups by utilizing modules to increase the self-esteem and decision-making processes for young ladies. This program was established for young ladies ages 8–14.

CB Ambassadors Program

Established for teen girls and women in multiple cities in the U.S. as well as internationally, CB Ambassadors are those who desire to make a difference in their communities by hosting two Consciously Beautiful Empowerment Sessions using the CB curriculum provided, as well as making appearances in their city at events that are created to empower women. CB Ambassadors are models for the Consciously Beautiful Movement and spread the Consciously Beautiful message through social media and their networks.

It is my hope that you, the reader, will join me in this mission by sharing this valuable work with the women and girls in your lives. There is an uncanny sense of freedom that comes with self-acceptance. When we don't fall in love with ourselves, the alternative is bondage. I want women to feel free. With this freedom, I know we can change the world.

ALIMA ALBARI,
CREATIVE DIRECTOR

"Albari aims for perfection on and off set. She is the ultimate team member."

—ARDRE ORIE

Alima Albari is a graduate of the Carolina School of Broadcasting. She is the owner of the multi-media production company and booking agency Studio Ninetytwo. Alima started her own consulting/management firm in 2009 called ALIMA INDUSTRIES. She has produced several fashion shows, co-ordinated industry events, and directed high-end fashion photo shoots.

Alima is a recipient of the SEA Promoter of the Year Award and a 2009 Emmy winner for the Positive Xchange TV show.

KEVIN DUKES,
LEAD PHOTOGRAPHER

"Dukes is a true talent who is able to capture unique beauty. His eye reveals his attention to detail."

—ARDRE ORIE

Kevin Dukes is a freelance photographer, videographer, web designer, and graphic designer in the state of Texas. Mr. Dukes captures unique images and intricate details that often go unnoticed, leaving observers of his work in awe.

Dukes received his Bachelor's in Electronic Engineering from DeVry University. In 2001, he founded Kevin Dukes Photography and immediately began capturing priceless images for many esteemed families in Texas. To date, Kevin Dukes Photography works on a variety of projects with emphasis in the fashion and modeling industry.

His greatest desire in life is to leave a lasting legacy for his two sons.

Feel free to contact Kevin Dukes' and visit his online portfolio at www.kdukesphoto.com as well as his Twitter, @kdukesphoto, and Facebook page, www.facebook.com/KDukesPhotography.

ABOUT THE AUTHOR,
ARDRE ORIE

Through her work as an educator, mentor, entrepreneur, and author of *Consciously Beautiful: I Am Enough*, Ardre Orie has dedicated her life to empowering women. After teaching for six years and serving as an assistant principle for four years, she founded the Pink Wish Foundation, a 501(c)(3), to alleviate economic distress and self-destructive behaviors in girls ages 8–18, which currently provides services to over 500 families in Florida and Georgia. Her cosmetic lines I Love Me and I Love Me Organics seek to inspire new generations of girls to live consciously beautiful lifestyles and take a stand against media messages that demean and devalue women. In June of 2013, Orie furthered that goal by launching I Love Me Magazine, an online and print publication devoted to spreading the message that true beauty comes from within. You can learn more about Ardre Orie and her mission at her website www.iamArdreOrie.com.